SMART WORDS
READER

Life in the
Grassland

Christine A. Caputo

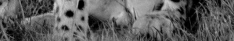
SCHOLASTIC INC.

What are SMART WORDS?

Smart Words are frequently used words that are essential to understanding topics taught in the classroom. The more Smart Words a child knows, the more easily he or she will grasp important curriculum concepts. Smart Words Readers introduce these key words in a fun, motivational format that promotes literacy skills. Each new Smart Word is highlighted, defined in context, and explored in greater detail. Engaging activities at the end of each chapter allow readers to practice the words they have learned.

Title page photo: A cheetah in the grassland

ISBN 978-0-545-59653-4

Packaged by Q2A Bill Smith

Series Editor: Nikki Bruno Clapper

Copyright © 2013 by Scholastic Inc.

Picture Credit: t= top, b= bottom, l= left, r= right, c= center

Cover Page: Michael L B Price/shutterstock, dgcampillo/Shutterstock(br).

Title Page: Stefanie Van Der Vinden/iStockphoto

Contents Page: Galyna Andrushko/Shutterstock

4: Igor Alyukov/Shutterstock; 5: Stanislav Spurny/Shutterstock; 6: Bob Stefko/ Botanica/Getty Images; 7: Mark R/Shutterstock; 8: pixbox77/Shutterstock(cl); 8–9: Elenamiv/Shutterstock; 9: Imageman/Shutterstock; 10: NattyPTG/Shutterstock; 11:NOAA/Science Photo Library; 13: Elzbieta Sekowska/Shutterstock; 14–15: Halstenbach/iStockphoto; 16: Nataliia Melnychuk/Shutterstock; 17: Chris Harris/All Canadas Photos/Glow Images; 18: SuperStock/Glow Images; 19: Yama/Shutterstock; 20: Johan Swanepoel/Shutterstock; 21: HHakim/iStockphoto(cr), Geoffrey Kuchera/ Shutterstock(b); 22: KaidoKarner/iStockphoto; 23: Designpics/Glow Images; 24–25: Dennis Donohue/Shutterstock; 25: Photoshot/India Pictures(tr); 26: serengeti130/ iStockphoto; 27: Juniors Bildarchiv/Juniors/Glow Images; 28: Igor Janicek/ Shutterstock; 29: David Steele/Shutterstock; 30: StevanZZ/Shutterstock.

Q2AMedia Art Bank: 7, 12.

12 11 10 9 8 7 6 5 4 3   13 14 15 16 17 18/0

Printed in the U.S.A.   40

First printing, September 2013

Table of Contents

Chapter 1

Seas of Grass

Wide-open land stretches as far as the eye can see. Golden fields bake in the afternoon sun. The ears and tail of a lioness are just visible over the thick grass.

What is this place? It must be the **grassland**!

If you answer yes to all of these questions, you're probably in a grassland!

- Is the ground covered in grass?
- Is the land flat or slightly hilly?
- Are there very few trees — or none at all?
- Are there both wet and dry seasons?

Wavy brown grass stretches as far as the eye can see in a Uganda grassland.

The grassland is one of Earth's major **biomes**. A biome is a community of plants and animals that live in a certain environment. Have you heard of the desert, the forest, and the tundra? These are biomes, too.

The grasslands of Argentina cover a vast area of land larger than the state of Texas. This region is called the pampas, which comes from a word meaning "flat land."

The grassland biome gets a medium amount of rainfall — between 20 and 50 inches (51 and 127 centimeters) each year. Most of the rain happens during one part of the year. This means the other part has a **drought**, or a period of little or no rain.

If grasslands got more rain, they would become forests. If they got less rain, they might be deserts. In fact, grasslands usually have forests on one side and deserts on the other.

SMART WORDS

grassland a biome that has flat land covered by grass, medium rainfall, and few or no trees

biome a community of plants and animals that share a certain environment

drought a period with little or no rain

From the Ground Up

As you can guess, grasslands are mostly filled with **grass**. There are more than 11,000 different kinds of grass. Some of them look like what you'd see in a lawn. But larger plants like wheat, rice, and oats are grasses, too.

Grasses are different from many other kinds of plants. They grow from the bottom instead of from the top. This helps them stay alive if something happens to parts above the ground. For instance, if an animal eats the grass, the plant can keep on growing from below.

Many of the native grasses of Kansas have fun common names. Have you heard of bottlebrush grass (shown here), big bluestem, goosegrass, hairy grama, and nimblewill?

The flowers of grasses grow from a **spikelet**. You might have seen this many-pointed structure on a wheat plant.

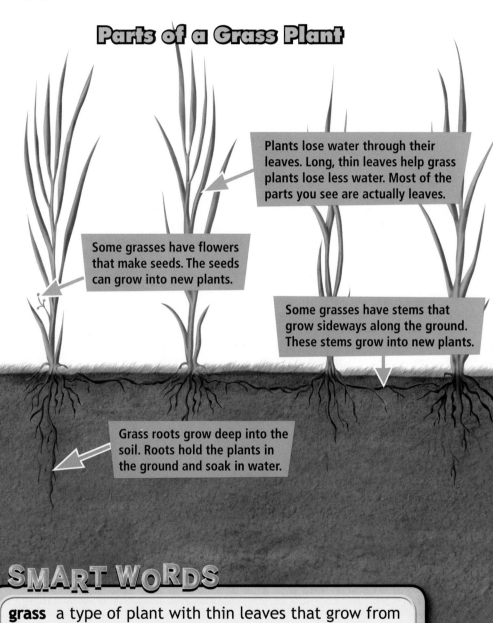

Parts of a Grass Plant

Plants lose water through their leaves. Long, thin leaves help grass plants lose less water. Most of the parts you see are actually leaves.

Some grasses have flowers that make seeds. The seeds can grow into new plants.

Some grasses have stems that grow sideways along the ground. These stems grow into new plants.

Grass roots grow deep into the soil. Roots hold the plants in the ground and soak in water.

SMART WORDS

grass a type of plant with thin leaves that grow from the bottom up

spikelet the part of a grass plant where flowers grow

A Biome That Feeds Millions

You might not live in or near grasslands, but you almost certainly rely on them. Grass plants are used for food all over the world. If you eat rice, corn, or oats, they were probably grown in grasslands. Other grass plants are used to make sugar, bread, and even plastic. Grasslands are also home to many domestic animals, such as cattle and sheep.

If you ever doubt the usefulness of grasslands, think of this fact: about three-quarters of grain products in the United States are made from the flour of one grass plant — wheat.

SMART WORD

erosion the movement of pieces of rock, sand, and soil from one place to another due to wind and water

Securing the Soil

Grassland plants are important in another way. They prevent, or at least slow down, the **erosion** of soil. Erosion happens when wind or water carries bits of soil from one place to another. Erosion can wear away soil. New soil takes many years to form. The roots of grasses help hold soil in place. This is especially important during droughts, when wind can easily move dusty soil.

Land can fall apart due to erosion. Here, you can see that grass holds soil in place, while the soil that was stripped of grass has worn away.

Use your SMART WORDS

Read each clue. Choose the Smart Word it describes.

grassland biome drought grass erosion

1. I am the process of carrying bits of soil to new places.

2. I am a group of plants and animals living in a certain place.

3. I am a long period of very little or no rain.

4. I am an area of flat land covered by grasses.

5. I am a plant with long, thin leaves that grow from the bottom up.

Answers on page 32

Talk Like a Scientist

Someone has asked you why grasslands are important. Use your Smart Words to tell what grasslands are and why they need to be protected.

SMART FACTS

Did You Know?

In the 1930s, a large area of American grasslands turned to dust due to a long drought, soil erosion, and poor farming methods. This area became known as the Dust Bowl.

That's Amazing!

Dry soil blew around in big storms. It made the sky look dark. The dust storms became known as black blizzards.

A National Menace?

In April 1935, the U.S. Congress declared that soil erosion was a national menace. The word *menace* is a strong way to say that something is a danger or a threat. The whole country was worried about the Dust Bowl because there wasn't enough soil for planting food crops.

Chapter 2

From Savanna to Prairie

Depending on where you are in the world, grasslands have different characteristics and go by different names. For example, in large parts of Africa you'll find low, grassy hills with a few trees scattered here and there. This describes the land in a **tropical** grassland. The word *tropical* describes places near the equator that are warm all year long. Tropical grasslands are also known as **savannas**.

Grasslands Around the World

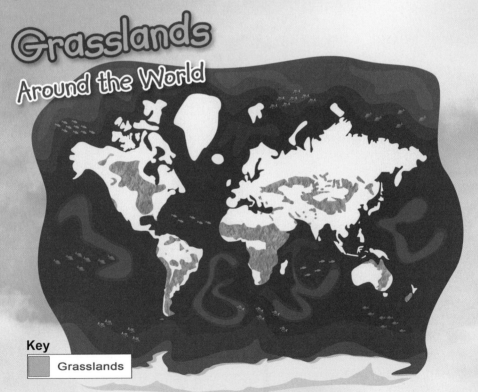

Key

Grasslands

About one-fourth of Earth's land is covered by grasslands. You can find them on every continent except Antarctica.

Fire is common on the savanna. During times of drought, the plants get very dry and stop growing. If a fire starts, it can spread quickly. Sometimes, lightning starts a fire naturally. Other times, humans cause fires to start. Either way, fires burn plants above the ground. This keeps many tall trees from growing on the savanna. But grasses have an advantage: since they grow from the bottom, they can grow back after a fire.

SMART WORDS

tropical warm, moist, and near the equator

savanna a tropical grassland

A fire sweeps across a grassland in Australia. This grass will take some time to recover and then grow back.

Gentler Grasslands

Grasslands grow in cooler parts of the world, too. Temperate grasslands grow farther from the equator than tropical grasslands do. The word *temperate* describes places that usually don't have weather extremes. They have hot summers and cold winters, but they don't get as hot as tropical areas or as cold as polar regions. They get slightly less rain than tropical grasslands, so instead of having a few trees here and there, they have none.

The steppes of Mongolia in northeastern China are temperate grasslands. They are covered by miles and miles of short grasses.

Some temperate grasslands have short grasses that never grow more than about 20 inches (50 centimeters) high. These are found in drier places. Other temperate grasslands have tallgrass that can be more than 6.5 feet (2 meters) tall. Grasses usually grow taller in places where they get more rain.

Regional Names of Temperate Grasslands

Name	Location
Prairies	North America
Steppes	Russia and Asia
Pampas	South America
Velds	South Africa

SMART WORD

temperate describing a region that does not have extremes of heat and cold

Humans and Grasslands

People sometimes create their own grassland biomes. The soil in some regions is very rich, or **fertile**. Because plants grow so well in these areas, people have cleared large areas of trees and other tall plants to make grasslands. Sometimes people start fires to burn down the trees. Other times they let animals feed on the plants.

Once the land is clear, people grow crops or raise animals. This use of land is known as **agriculture**.

The invention of plows and tractors made it even easier for people to use grasslands for agriculture.

Unfortunately, people are also harming grasslands. Sometimes they clear *all* of the plants in a certain area to build homes and businesses. Human settlements replace the natural grassland biome.

Changes in climate can affect grasslands, too. Human activities may be causing the overall climate on Earth to get warmer. This can change which areas get rain. Grasslands could transform into different biomes.

SMART WORDS

fertile filled with nutrients that plants need to grow

agriculture the process of growing crops or raising animals for food

Large areas of grassland are being destroyed every day to make way for human activity.

Use your SMART WORDS

Answer each question with a Smart Word.

tropical	savanna	temperate
fertile		agriculture

1. Which term describes soil that is rich in nutrients for growing plants?
2. Which term describes growing crops or raising animals?
3. Which term describes an area that does not have extreme heat or cold?
4. Which term is another name for a tropical grassland?
5. Which term describes areas near the equator?

Answers on page 32

Talk Like a Scientist

A friend from a tropical grassland and a friend from a temperate grassland send letters to each other. Use your Smart Words to write a sentence from each friend to describe his or her grassland.

SMART FACTS

Did You Know?

More than 99 percent of North America's prairie lands are used for agriculture — growing crops. That means only 1 percent of the original American prairies are left untouched.

Prairie Pimples

The prairie is extremely flat. Its low hills are called pimples, and the tallest ones are only about 4 feet (1.5 meters) high.

Deeply Rooted

The roots of North American prairie grasses can be 15 feet (4.6 meters) deep. This helps the prairie survive fires, grass-eating animals, and long periods without rain.

Chapter 3

Alive in the Grass

Grasslands around the world are home to a wide variety of animals. Grass itself can be a major source of food. Animals that eat only plants are called **herbivores**. Grassland herbivores range from tiny to gigantic — from grasshoppers to deer-like impalas to huge African elephants.

Elephants have six pairs of molars during their lives. These brick-size teeth are great for grinding tough grass and other plants.

Giraffes are also herbivores. They use their long tongues to pluck leaves from trees. They can also bend down to pull leaves from lower plants. Animals that feed on leaves and twigs are called **browsers**.

Many other grassland herbivores are **grazers**. They feed on grasses and other plants along the ground. The American bison is a grazer.

Giraffes are the tallest animals in the world. They can reach up to 19 feet (6 meters).

Bison are herbivores found on the American prairies.

Grassland Hunters

A mighty lion sits at the top of a grass-covered hill on the African savanna. This cat is searching for her next meal. Lions and other **carnivores** eat only meat. They must hunt and catch their food.

Grassland carnivores often hunt herbivores. Many people are surprised to learn that female lions usually do the hunting.

A group of lions, called a pride, often works together to catch zebras, antelopes, or gazelles. Lions rest for as long as twenty hours a day. They use the other few hours to hunt and to eat.

Coyotes roam in temperate grasslands of North and Central America. They have great eyesight and a strong sense of smell. A coyote can stalk another animal by following it without being seen. Then, once it gets close, it pounces on the animal.

Coyotes eat rabbits, mice, snakes, and even insects. They eat mostly meat, but they eat fruit and other plant parts, too. An animal that eats both meat and plants is called an **omnivore**.

SMART WORDS

carnivore an animal that feeds only on other animals

omnivore an animal that feeds on both plants and animals

Coyotes usually hunt alone, but sometimes they hunt in groups called packs.

The Need for Speed

In some biomes there are plenty of places for animals to hide — but not in grasslands. There are no big trees or rocks. There are just open fields. Some animals can't hide, so they have to run fast to stay alive.

Prey are animals that are hunted by other animals for food. They run away from **predators** — the animals that hunt them. Gazelles are common prey. They run up to 65 miles (105 kilometers) per hour to escape predators.

SMART WORDS

prey an animal that is hunted and eaten

predator an animal that hunts and eats other animals

A common predator of the gazelle is the cheetah. These big cats have long, strong legs. A cheetah can reach a speed of 60 miles (96 kilometers) per hour in just 3 seconds. That's faster than most cars!

When a predator gets close, a gazelle sometimes leaps straight into the air. Scientists think this might help the gazelle stop its attacker.

Cheetahs have excellent eyesight. They look around to spot their prey, and when the time is right, they use their swift speed to catch it. This cheetah is chasing a warthog.

Hiding in Plain Sight

Many grassland animals have fur or skin color that blends in with their surroundings. This is known as camouflage. Smaller animals, like prairie dogs, tend to be mostly one solid color, such as tan or green. This makes it hard to see them against the ground or the grass.

Large grazing animals often have patterns of colors. Zebras have a striped pattern. The stripes on a group of zebras can be confusing. This makes it hard for a predator to pick out one zebra to hunt.

Can you count the zebras? A lion probably can't, either. This may cause the lion to give up and find other food.

The black-footed ferret doesn't dig its own burrows. It steals burrows from prairie dogs.

Some animals hide by burrowing. They use sharp claws or teeth to dig underground holes and tunnels. Ground squirrels and prairie dogs are burrowing prey animals. Weasels and ferrets are burrowing predators. That means no one is safe, even underground!

Predator or prey, tall or short grass, the animals and plants of the grassland biome share a special environment. The next time you see a field that seems to go on forever, imagine what hides in those blades of grass.

SMART WORDS

camouflage colors or patterns that help an animal blend in with its background

burrow to dig a hole or tunnel underground

Match each description to the correct Smart Word.

herbivore	browser	grazer
carnivore	omnivore	prey
predator	camouflage	burrow

1. to dig a hole or tunnel in the ground
2. an animal that eats both plants and meat
3. an herbivore that eats grasses and other plants along the ground
4. a pattern or color that helps an animal blend in to its environment
5. an animal that is hunted and eaten
6. an herbivore that eats leaves and twigs
7. an animal that eats only plants
8. an animal that eats only meat
9. an animal that hunts other animals for food

Answers on page 32

Talk Like a Scientist

Somebody shows you a picture of animals in the African savanna. Use your Smart Words to write captions about the different kinds of grassland animals.

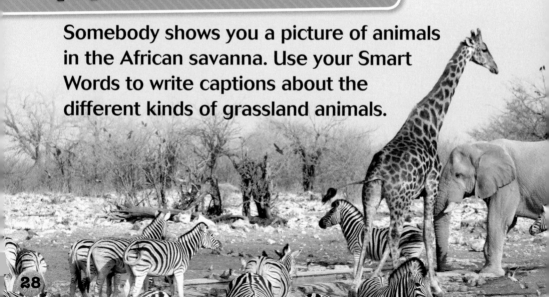

SMART FACTS

That's a Lot!

African elephants eat grass, leaves, bark, and roots. An adult elephant can eat 300 to 400 pounds (136 to 181 kilograms) of plants every day.

That's Amazing!

Elephants can fill their trunks with several gallons of water. Then they squirt it into their mouths.

Did You Know?

Elephants can "talk" to each other. Some of their sounds are too low for humans to hear.

Glossary

agriculture the process of growing crops or raising animals for food

biome a community of plants and animals that share a certain environment

browser an herbivore that feeds on leaves and twigs

burrow to dig a hole or tunnel underground

camouflage colors or patterns that help an animal blend in with its background

carnivore an animal that feeds only on other animals

drought a period with little or no rain

erosion the movement of pieces of rock, sand, and soil from one place to another due to wind and water

fertile filled with nutrients that plants need to grow

grass a type of plant with thin leaves that grow from the bottom up

grassland a biome that has flat land covered by grass, medium rainfall, and few or no trees

grazer an herbivore that feeds on grasses and other plants close to the ground

herbivore an animal that feeds only on plants

omnivore an animal that feeds on both plants and animals

predator an animal that hunts and eats other animals

prey an animal that is hunted and eaten

savanna a tropical grassland

spikelet the part of a grass plant where flowers grow

temperate describing a region that does not have extremes of heat and cold

tropical warm and near the equator

Index

SMART WORDS Answer Key

p. 10

1. erosion, 2. biome, 3. drought, 4. grassland, 5. grass

p. 18

1. fertile, 2. agriculture, 3. temperate, 4. savanna, 5. tropical

p. 28

1. burrow, 2. omnivore, 3. grazer, 4. camouflage, 5. prey, 6. browser, 7. herbivore, 8. carnivore, 9. predator